DIARY OF A
MYSTIC

BONNIE TEMPLETON

ISBN: 979-8-9876509-0-5 (paperback) | 979-8-9876509-1-2 (ebook)
Library of Congress Control Number: 2023903268
BISAC: RELIGION / Mysticism; RELIGION / Spirituality

Book design: Peggy Nehmen, www.n-kcreative.com
Printed in the United States of America.

Published by Bonnie Templeton.
St. Louis, Missouri

TABLE OF CONTENTS

Introduction

LET ME BEGIN BY saying this book is not a scholarly work nor is it an autobiography. It is truly a diary of my mystical experiences. Originally, I started to write about my experiences for my children (now middle-aged men). I wanted them to know about my spiritual journey.[1] Perhaps, my grandchildren will be interested in my experiences when they grow up.

I have found that as one grows, it is necessary to jettison one's image of G1d[2] that no longer works and formulate a new view of G1d over time. This new view will fit for a while before it too needs to be reimagined. For example, most children outgrow the image of G1d as an old man with a long white beard sitting on a throne. As they near 10 years old, sometimes they substitute the idea that G1d can be found in Nature. Others simply substitute a question mark when asked about their ideas of G1d. This process continues as we mature first one idea and then another. In between ideas

---

1 In the biblical narrative, patriarchs describe their experiences with G1d to their children. For example, Jacob tells Joseph that *El Shaddai had appeared to him and blessed him (Genesis 48:3).*

2 In Judaism it is forbidden to misuse G1d's name. Therefore, I have chosen to use a one instead of an "o" when writing the word G-d. I chose the number "1" to emphasize that G1d is one.

about G1d, we may become agnostics or atheists, which brings me to the second reason for writing this book.

In our world, there are many views about G1d and religion. Some people are strict followers of a religion and others are profound atheists. This book may not be for them. This book is for people of faith as well as those people who have rational doubts about the existence of a deity but would like to believe that G1d exists.

We learn about G1d in two ways: 1) we believe someone who has had a personal experience or 2) we have a personal experience ourselves. I have been fortunate enough to have had several personal experiences.

I have always felt a spiritual pull, although as a child I did not know, nor could I name this pull. When I was seven, I wanted to go to church with a friend—to be with her or with G1d—I could not say. My parents explained that we were Jewish, and Jews did not go to church.

When I was eight, my parents could not care for my brother and me because of illness and divorce. We were sent to boarding school. There, I experienced church services. There was something about them that satisfied a yearning inside me. Now I would name that "something" as spiritual longing. One Sunday when I was nine, a teacher asked us "who would like to light candles before the service." I put my hand up right away, which was very unusual for me because usually I asked to go second rather than first. I was delighted to be part of the service. When we were reunited with our mother and our new stepfather, we were introduced to Jewish education and Jewish services. My first mystical experience occurred when I was 13 and will be described in Chapter Two.

▪ ▪ ▪

The chapters are written in the following format. First, I describe the spiritual experience. Sometimes the description of an experience is accompanied by poetry or an artistic depiction of the experience. After I describe the experience, I discuss any lesson I learned from it and how the experience affected my life.

After 60 years of sporadic spiritual experiences, I have come to understand that there is a fifth dimension in addition to the four that everybody knows (length, width, height, time). I call this dimension the spiritual dimension. It is through this dimension that we connect to G1d and everything in the world. Each of us has a spark of G1d within us, which allows us to connect with the spiritual dimension. Many people call this spark a "soul."

Living in the material world it is easy to cover our soul with the needs and worries of life. The thicker the covering, the harder it is to perceive the spark of G1d that is within us, so, we come to believe that it does not exist. Physical illness or emotional distress make it much harder to connect with the spark of G1d within us. I am unable to feel G1d's presence when I am sick or in pain. I wrote the following poem a few years ago but forgot to date it.

I AM A SPARK OF G1D

My purpose is to let the spirit of G1d
shine through me by being:

Loving

Caring

Helpful

And feeling the wonder of all things.

2

Blue Angel

IN MARCH OF 1960, when I was 13 years old, I had an appendectomy. Back then the incision was four inches long and required a week's stay in the hospital. I was on the pediatric floor of the hospital, but my surgeon only had standing orders for painkillers on the surgical floor. It was the first time in my life that I knew real pain, and I have been afraid of real pain ever since. However, there was nothing odd in that experience.

The odd experience came a few days later when I had a unique vision. Perhaps I was asleep or perhaps I was in a state between wakefulness and sleep. I saw a male angel dressed in a sky-blue robe. This angel was leaning out of a background of off-white concentric circles with his arms outstretched toward me. His hair was shoulder length, smooth, silky and vivid white. I was afraid and woke up; I said to my mother, who was sitting by my bed, "Mommy, Mommy I am going to die." I told her what I had experienced, and she suggested that perhaps the angel was there to make sure that I did not die. I found her suggestion comforting then and now even after 63 years. I refer to him as "blue angel" and have seen him on other occasions, so, I have come to regard him as my guardian angel. Blue angel did not look like any image of an angel that I had ever seen; first he was male, second his hair was not like human hair in color or texture and third his hair was shoulder-length. (This was way before the Beatles). The picture below is my drawing of blue angel as he appeared to me when I was 13 years old. This drawing was done 60 years later.

The next time I saw blue angel was on January 11, 1981, the day before I was to enter the hospital for prophylactic bilateral mastectomies. I was having this surgery because all the women in my family had died of breast cancer, and I knew that I was at very high risk for the disease. Also, I had two young children ages one and almost four, and I did not want to leave them motherless. In September of 1980, my obstetrician had found a large lump in my breast which needed to be removed. Several other lumps had appeared in the ensuing months, so it seemed like a good idea to have my breasts removed—one last biopsy to end all biopsies.

On the afternoon of January 11, 1981, I was resting on my bed somewhere between sleep and wakefulness when Blue Angel appeared to me again. He took my hand and led me to three glowing forms standing in front of a black void. They were beautiful but not human—no arms or legs; they seemed to be made up of glowing diamond shapes. They told me that I had suffered enough for two lifetimes and I could die. When I awoke, I said goodbye to all things on earth except my sons. I could not say goodbye to them. During the surgery two days later, I almost died twice. Once on the operating table and once in the recovery room. Needless to say, I do not remember the time during the operation, however, I do remember the incident in the recovery room. I remember fighting my way to consciousness and growling at the doctors that they had better do something because they were losing me. Then I slipped back into unconsciousness again. The next day, one of the doctors at whom I had growled came to visit and explained that I had almost died then.

Sometime later I wrote a poem describing my experience with the three glowing forms.

REBIRTH

Dressed in blue, the angel came
And took me by the hand
To meet three glowing forms
Alive with diamonds shifting,
Changing, yet remaining,
They stood before a blackened void;
Gently they reviewed my life
Before inviting me.
Please, my children are too young
To be without a mother's hand
As they mature to men.
I choose this life
Where pain and joy are lovers
Content to feel
And lend my strength to others.

Thankful, I awoke
And instead of death
Found new meaning in life.

THREE GLOWING FORMS

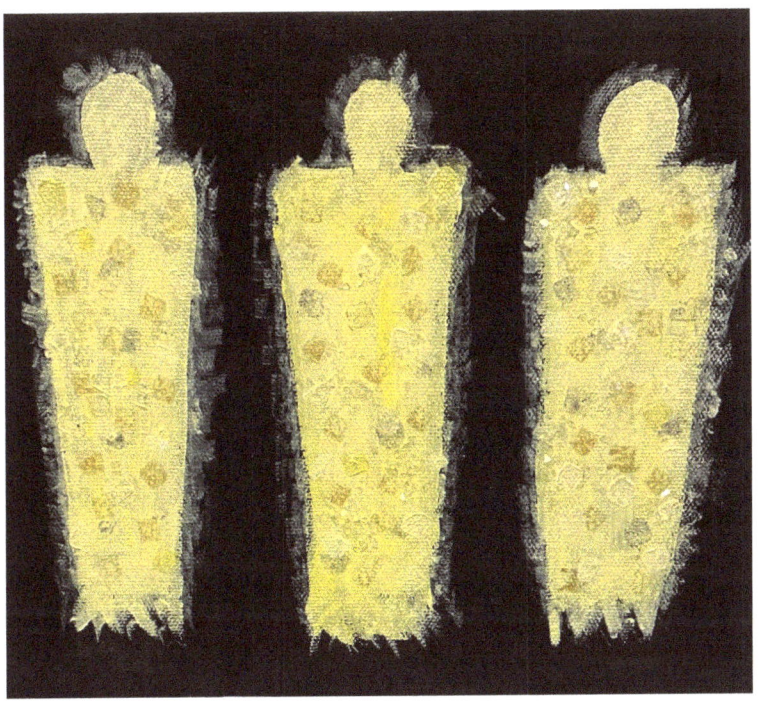

■ ■ ■

My life changed radically after Blue Angel took me to meet the three glowing forms. I felt like my life had been handed to me on a silver platter. For the first time in a long while, I felt like I had a future rather than dying young from breast cancer. I also thought (incorrectly) that there would be no more suffering. While there were certainly more difficult times in my life, I also knew that I would be able to raise my sons to adulthood and that was the greatest of all gifts.

Another way my life changed was my markedly increased desire to help other people. At the time I was working part time in a biochemistry lab. I enjoyed the work, especially analyzing data. However, it was not meeting my new need to help others. At the same time, I was in therapy to deal with some issues from my childhood, so I decided to enroll in social work school and become a therapist.

Two things happened in social work school. One, I learned that I had become enmeshed with my therapist, and two, I met DCN. The first time I saw her, something inside me jumped; it seemed that a part of me recognized her at some level. She told me that she had the same experience. Now, I would say that our souls recognized each other. Throughout our long friendship, we discussed theology together many times. In spite of practicing different religions, our views about theology were very similar. We concluded that our souls came from the same soul-pod.

Many years later, I met a woman in Israel who I think is also a member of my soul pod. Like DCN and myself, she is a teacher and is very religious. She worked at a college instructing student teachers how to teach English. During her classes, she would weave in religious teachings to secular Israeli and Arab students.

■ ■ ■

The next time I saw blue angel was on an airplane flying to Israel when my husband was in intensive care at Rambam Hospital in Haifa. He was hospitalized for Ludwig's Angina between January 29 and February 5 2003. To make this story make sense, let's start at the beginning.

I no longer remember how long we were in Israel at that time, perhaps a month. Alan had a tooth worked on before we left home, and it was still sore some weeks later when we flew to Israel. I was concerned about his pain and suggested he go back to the dentist. Of course, he did not take my advice and we traveled to Israel in December of 2002. Alan had scientific collogues in Israel with whom he collaborated. I was preparing to teach a spring semester biology course at Washington University in St. Louis; so, while Alan was busy at the Rambam, I used their library to update my lectures. All of the time in Haifa, Alan's tooth was still sore and he planned to see the dentist when he returned to St. Louis. I returned to St. Louis before Alan, because I had to start teaching my class.

The day he was scheduled to return home, his physician friends noticed that he was not well and took him to see one of their collogues at the hospital. He was admitted to the hospital and diagnosed with Ludwig's Angina, which is a dangerous infection that is usually fatal. Our Israeli friends visited him and kept me appraised of the situation. In the beginning of his hospitalization, he was doing well; then, he took a turn for the worse. The first hint I had that something was wrong with Alan was a strange vision that occurred at the end of *Shabbat*³ morning services at synagogue. In the vision, I saw both of my grandmothers standing by a stretcher with a body on it. The vision was frightening because both of my grandmothers had been widowed before they had died. Our Israeli friends had gone to visit Alan after *Shabbat* was over and were told that he was in intensive care. They called me first thing Sunday morning.

Meanwhile, Alan called me Saturday night my time and early Sunday morning Israeli time. He could barely talk but explained that he had thought that he would not live to see the morning. He called me when he saw the dawn. After I

---

3   *Shabbat* is the Hebrew word for the sabbath.

heard about his night, I asked him if he wanted me to come to Israel. He said that he did not want me to come. He called several more times after that. I checked on flights to Israel for the next day (Sunday) but did not buy a ticket. I wanted to go but he kept saying no.

I really was torn about going to Israel because Alan kept saying not to come but our Israeli friends thought that I should make the trip. Finally, I sat on the couch, emptied my mind and prayed for advice. Within 30 seconds the phone rang — it was Alan asking me to come to Israel. I had never gotten to the front of the prayer queue before nor have I since.

Now there were many arrangements to be made. I tried to buy my plane ticket on line but could not because it was less than five hours before the flight, so I had to call Continental Airlines[4] to make my reservations. Then I had to find someone to teach my class for the week. Within a few hours, I was at the airport. Because I had made the reservations so close to the time of departure, my boarding pass was stamped with big red letters to ensure that I would be searched. In spite of the glaring red letters on my boarding pass, no one asked a question or searched me or my luggage. It was as though I was invisible!

In Newark when I boarded the plane to Israel, I recognized one of the flight attendants whom I had seen on other flights to or from Israel. I explained to him that I had not been able to order a kosher meal because I had made my reservation so late. I asked him if he could give me a kosher meal after he had served everyone who had ordered one. The flight attendant served me a kosher meal first; when I protested, he said

---

4 Continental Airlines merged with United Airlines in 2010.

he knew I always ate a kosher meal. I was delighted because I had not eaten that day.

After a while I noticed Blue Angel sitting in the seat next to me. I was surprised and asked him if he didn't have a faster way of getting to Israel than by plane. We did make the trip from Newark to Tel Aviv in 9.5 hours, which is the fastest I have ever made the trip! I was met by a driver to take me to the hospital in Haifa. Blue Angel rode with me, and we were accompanied by another angel who was dressed in red and was above and a little behind our car. Both angels were gone by the time we arrived at Rambam hospital.

Eventually, Alan fully recovered from Ludwig's Angina. At the time the physicians who treated him were sure he would die, which was the usual outcome for these cases. Actually, the physicians of the Dental Surgery Department invited Alan to attend its annual meeting as the "miracle patient of the year."

When Alan read this chapter about Blue Angel, he asked me how I communicated with Blue Angel. The reality is that Blue Angel has not spoken to me. If I ask a question, I think the words but I do not knowingly get a response.

3

Shavuot

CONFIRMATION 1962

SHAVUOT IS THE JEWISH holiday that commemorates the giving of the ten commandments at Mt. Sinai. It also marks 50 days from the second day of Passover. On the second day of Passover an *omer*[5] of new barley was offered at the Temple. This event marked the beginning of the barley harvest. Jews count 49 days (7 weeks) after the *omer* was offered to arrive at the holiday of *Shavuot*.

I was raised as a Reform Jew in Cincinnati, Ohio, which was the center of Reform Judaism at that time. Back then the ceremony of Confirmation had replaced the Bar/Bat Mitzvah ceremony. Confirmation was held on Shavuot and marked the end of 10th grade and formal religious school education. Everyone wore graduation type gowns—the boys wore blue and the girls wore white. The girls carried baskets of flowers that were placed on the *bima* (raised platform) for decoration. All of us walked down the center aisle of the sanctuary which had been decorated with hoops of flowers. It was quite an elaborate and very moving ceremony. Each of us gave a

---

5 An *omer* is a measure of dry goods

short speech that we had written—mine was on the sixth commandment, you shall not murder. Toward the end of the ceremony each of us approached the rabbis by the open ark for words of wisdom and a blessing. I no longer remember what the rabbis said, but I do remember it was meaningful to me. Because Confirmation was such an important rite of passage, we received plenty of presents, and there was a reception in the evening.

On a Friday evening about two weeks before Confirmation, there was a private service for the confirmands and their parents. After the service, the confirmands received two sheets of paper. On one sheet was the decalogue, in English, and on the other sheet was a Declaration of Faith. We were told to memorize the words on both pages, because we would recite them in unison. I did not mind memorizing the pages, however, I had serious qualms about saying the Declaration of Faith. I was being asked to promise that I would always be Jewish.

Here was my problem: when I was a very young child, my parents told me that I was Jewish, but I had no clue about what being Jewish meant. When I was seven, my parents divorced and my mother had a nervous breakdown. My grandmother sent my younger brother and me to boarding school on the East Coast. We spent a year and a half away from family. While we were at boarding school, we went to church every Sunday with all of the other children. Going to church satisfied something inside me although I had no name for it at the time. (Now I would call it my soul).

So here I was two weeks before Confirmation being asked to pledge that I would be Jewish always. I could not make the promise with integrity, because I had been comfortable in church services; so, I raised my hand and asked the rabbi if the Declaration of Faith was binding. Needless to say, my question was not well received by the rabbi or my mom and stepdad.

When we got home, I told my mom and stepdad that I did not want to be confirmed, because I did not want to say the Declaration of Faith. They gave me a choice: I could be confirmed or be grounded for a long time. I chose to go through the ceremony, but still I had a problem with the Declaration of Faith. I memorized it along with everything else we were told to memorize, but I did not want the statement to be binding for me. When the moment came to recite the Declaration of Faith, I slipped my hand behind my back and crossed my fingers. It was my way of telling G1d that I needed more time to explore other religions, which I did for the next 18 years.

During these years, I was able to pray comfortably in any church or synagogue. I visited mosques as a tourist but I did not feel the need to pray in any of them. I even went to Buddha Day services in Hawaii, and thought they were very similar to church services. That same year, I had the opportunity to see an exhibition of Thai Buddhas, where I felt the most profound sense of peace. I also read a number of books about various religions. Throughout these years, I maintained my Jewish identity by going to Hillel for the Jewish holidays. After meeting the three glowing forms before my mastectomies, I felt a much stronger spiritual pull. In response to this pull I began going to my neighbor's church and I joined a group of Jews thinking about founding a new congregation. This two-pronged effort to meet my spiritual needs lasted until I had an amazing dream.

THE DREAM 1984

Twenty-two years after my confirmation, I signed up for a Biblical Hebrew course taught at Washington University. I asked the professor if I could sit in on his course without registering, and therefore, not paying the enrollment fee. The professor was very generous and said, "Yes, as long as you do all of the homework and take the exams." This was a great deal and I will be forever grateful to this generous professor.

About three weeks after the start of the semester, between the holidays of *Rosh Hashanah*[6] and *Yom Kippur,*[7] I had a most remarkable dream. I dreamt that I was reading from G1d's *Torah.*[8] I say G1d's *Torah* because the *eitz hayim* were not wood, instead, they were made of a gleaming, glittering, glistening, golden material. After I read from the *Torah*, I gave a speech about the Ten Commandments and said the Declaration of Faith <u>without</u> my fingers crossed. At this point in my Hebrew education, I had learned the Hebrew letters and a few words. I had never seen the inside of a *Torah*, and yet in this dream I was reading *Torah*. The speech that I gave in the dream was about the Ten Commandments, so I guessed that I was reading the *Torah* portion for *Shavuot.*[9] I looked up the *Torah* portion for *Shavuot* in an orthodox prayer

---

6 *Rosh Hashanah* is the Jewish New Year.

7 *Yom Kippur* is the Day of Atonement where one seeks forgiveness for one's sins

8 The *Torah* contains the first five books in the Hebrew Bible. It is written on parchment that is attached to two wooden rollers called *eitz hayim*. Notice that I had to enroll in a Hebrew class before I had the dream—that is to say that I had to take the first step!

9 *Shavuot* is the Jewish holiday that commemorates the giving of the Ten Commandments

book; when I went to the listed pages, I found two pages in Hebrew only. As I scanned through the pages, I came across the words that I had read in the dream! Then, I looked up the Ten Commandments in a *Chumash*.[10] There again, I found the Hebrew words that I had read in the *Torah*. After finding the words that I had read in my dream, I wrote down as much of the speech as I could remember. Some of it I remembered verbatim, some of it I remembered major themes and some of it I just remembered the topics. The rabbi in the dream was from New York; he was the rabbi who had come to St. Louis to lead services for *Rosh Hashanah* and *Yom Kippur*. It was clear from the dream that I was to have a *Bat Mitzvah* on *Shavuot* under the tutelage of this rabbi. It took me two months to get up the nerve to call the rabbi and ask him to help me prepare for a *Bat Mitzvah*.

The rabbi was very gracious and agreed to take me on as a student. I was taking Biblical Hebrew and I thought that would be enough, however, I was mistaken. Rabbi BG guided me through two books[11] and three tractates of *Talmud*[12] in English. I found the reading educational and valuable. At some point Rabbi BG asked to see a draft of my speech. I had hoped to be able to give it from my notes and not write it down—so much for hopes. In actuality there was a valuable lesson to be learned by writing down my *Devar Torah* [commentary on the Torah portion]. When Rabbi BG returned my speech to

---

10 A *Chumash* is a book that contains the first five books of the Hebrew Bible—Genesis, Exodus, Leviticus, Numbers and Deuteronomy.

11 *Back to the Sources: Reading the Classic Jewish Texts* by Barry W. Holtz; *As a Driven Leaf* by Milton Steinberg

12 Bava Kamma, Bava Metzia and Bava Basra

me, some portions had no red marks at all, whereas, others were covered in red. What was interesting to me was that the parts I had written down verbatim from the dream had NO red marks! The commandments that had no red marks dealt with the relationship between G1d and human beings. What is surprising to me, about my commentary on these commandments is how dated they are. They were meant for a specific group of people at a specific time. So to, the Torah was meant for a specific group of people at a specific time, therefore, it is not surprising that some of it seems antiquated to us. I interpreted this dream as a message from G1d that it was time for me to be Jewish and to stop attending church, which I did. This was a message for me on how I was to live my life rather than any message about the church I had been attending. I have included this speech on the following pages for those who wish to read it. Feel free to skip this speech and proceed to Standing at Sinai on page 30.

Shavuot 5745   Sunday 26 May 1985

INTRODUCTION

—Why now?

1. Shavuot is anniversary of confirmation

    a. reservations because when I was 15, I had not yet studied comparitive religion and philosophy

    b. did not feel comfortable making a declaration of faith.

2. Dream in September

3. Comments re: Shavuot & Decalogue

Shavuot commemorates the giving of the 10 commandments to Moses and the children of Israel. It was the revelation at Mt. Sinai that forged the hebrew slaves into a people. A people unified by their belief in one universal God and the laws given by that God. Let us examine these laws and the way in which they can be applied today.

The first 4 commandments deal with our relationship with God and the remaining 6 commandments deal with our relationships with each other.

THE DECALOGUE

1. I am the Lord your God who brought you from the land of Egypt from the house of bondage.

This commandment is a statement that both identifies God and gives the hebrew people the reason they should obey the remaining commandments. It leaves no doubt that it was God who enabled the slaves to go free, rather than Moses working alone. Essentially, God is saying: you saw me free you from

Egypt with your own eyes, therefore, believe in me, trust in me and obey me. This statement is not unlike the story that Gary told on Rosh Hashana in which faith was compared to climbing into a wheelbarrow to be ferried across a waterfall via a tightrope after seeing the feat performed. It is very scary to have faith. On the other hand, there is a positive aspect to having faith which is illustrated in a scene from the movie "Star Wars". The Empire Strikes Back After Luke has tried unsuccessfully to raise his X-wing fighter from a swamp on Dagoba, Yoda raises the fighter. Luke murmers "I don't believe it" and Yoda replies "that is why you fail."

2. You shall not have other gods before me. You shall not make for you an idol or any form that is in the sky above or the earth below or the sea below the land. You shall not bow down to them and you shall not serve them because I, the Lord your God, am a zealous God who visits the iniquity of the parents upon the children, upon the third generation and upon the forth generation for the ones who hate me. And doing kindness to the thousandth generation for those who love me and keep my commandments.

This commandment taken together with the first commandment implies that God should be first in our lives. What does it mean to put God first in our lives? The answer is suggested by the last sentence of this commandment: to love God and to obey God's commandments. This commandment is necessitated by our propensity to make our own gods. If this were not so, there would have been no need to include the sentence 'you shall not make for you an idol or any form'. Some of the gods we forge today are: careers, money, fame or another person. When we act in such a way that we, ourselves, benefit at the expence of another person or by disregarding the mitzvot, we are putting something else before God--we are forging a false god. For instance, let's take an example that most of us will have to deal with at some time in our lives--our boss asks us to do something that is wrong according to the Ten commandments such as: fudging data, burying evidence, keeping two sets of books, sleeping with him or her. What do we do? It takes a lot of courage to say no to one's boss, after all no one wants to be fired. Putting God first means putting God's laws first and that means saying NO. I think this commandment, to have no other gods, is the most difficult to keep.

3.   Yor shall not take the name of the Lord your God for nothing because the Lord will not regard as innocent the one who will take his/her/it name for nothing.

The hebrew word which I translated as nothing is לַשָּׁוְא. It is a noun that the noted dictionary of biblical hebrew compiled by Brown, Driver and Briggs defines as emptiness, nothingness, worthlessness, vanity. With this information it is easy to see that God's name should be invoked only for serious, important reasons; it should not be invoked lightly. This meaning of the third commandment is considerably broader than just a prohibition against swearing. Rabbi Rosenbloom used the following anecdote to illustrate this point. A member of his congregation asked him to pray that it would not rain on is daughter's wedding day. Rabbi Rosenbloom refused saying the weather was unimportant but he would be glad to pray for success of the marriage.

4.   Remember the sabbath day to keep it holy. Six days you

shall labor and do all your work and the seventh day will be a sabbath to the Lord your God. On it you shall not do any work, nor your son, nor your daughter, nor your manservant, nor your maidservant, nor your animals, nor the soujourner who is within your gates. Because in six days the Lord made the heaven and the earth, the sea and all that is in them but on the seventh day the Lord rested. Therefore, the Lord blessed the sabbath day and made it holy.

This commandment contains two ~~proscriptions~~ rules (regulations) for the sabbath day: 1)to do no work and 2)to keep the day holy. Furthermore, the commandment also precludes having other people or animals doing our work for us. The word shabbat in hebrew comes from the hebrew root שׁבת which means to cease. Thus, the sabbath day is the day one ceases from working. Doing no work on Saturday is not so easily done in our society, especially, when local laws require stores to remain closed on Sunday. Now that we have Sunday sales in St. Louis it is easier for us to rest on Saturday and do our errands on Sunday. The second part of the commandment enjoins us to keep the day holy. One way to make the day holy is by attending a worship service. Another way to make the day holy is by studying torah or subjects related to Judaism a part of our sabbath day.

The following midrash illustrates the essence of the sabbath day. R. Hiyya b. Abba was invited to share a sabbath meal with a man in Laodicea. They sat before a large table laden with items that had been created within the first six days--including a child. The child sat in the middle of the table and recited the first line of Psalm 24: "The earth is the Lord's and the fulness thereof". Why? to prevent the owner from growing conceited. R. Hiyya b. Abba asked the man

how he came to be so wealthy. The man replied:"I was a
butcher and whenever I saw a well-favored animal, I set it
aside for the sabbath.

Once observing the sabbath becomes a habit, the day
becomes delightful.

5. Honor your father and your mother in order that your days
will grow long upon the land that the Lord your God is giving
you.

This commandment is a tough one; one that I certainly do
not keep well. Before we examine hat this commandment says,
let's look at some of the reasons it is so difficult to keep.
1)When we were children, our parents thwarted many of our
wishes and plans. An action that was probably designed to
teach us right from wrong and/or keep us safe, but it also
left some resentment within us. 2)Sometimes our parents were
unreasonable with us just as we are sometimes unreasonable
with our children. 3)Sometimes our parents were not the
parents that we wanted them to be and we feel that they
failed us. This commandment really dosen't say anything
about our feelings towards our parents; it says we should
treat them with honor regardless of our feelings. The Random
House Unabridged Dictionary defines honor as respect and
esteem. What are some of the reasons that we are asked to
show them respect and esteem even if we are angry at them for
real or imagined hurts? 1)They raised us at great emotional
and financial expence. 2)As we try to do our best with our
children, they probably tried to do their best with us.
3)Nachmonides sugests that we honor our parents because they

assisted God in our formation. 4)Because God has commanded us to honor them and we attempt to do as God commands because God freed us from Egyptian slavery and gave us the land of Isreal. Speaking of Isreal, this is the only commandment that offers a specific reward for obedience--prolonging our days in Isreal. [Suggesting which to me that God knows how difficult it is for us to honor our parents.)

6. You shall not murder.

This commandment is concerned with murder--the premeditatied, willful taking of another person's life. It is not a ban on all killing. It does not prohibit killing in war or the death penalty.

7. You shall not commit adultery.

In biblical times, this commandment prohibited a married woman from having sexual relations with anyone other than her husband; but it only prohibited a man from having sexual relations with married women other than his wife. In those days men could have many wives and concubines. A well known example is King David; however, he was punished for commiting adultery with Uriah's wife. In those days, too, women were considered property. This point can be infered from Mishna 2a in Kiddushin which says that "a woman is acquired (in marriage) in three ways...by money, by deed, or by intercourse...And she acquires herself (ie is no longer married) by divorce or by her husband's death...." Note that a man married a woman when he had intercourse with her. And a woman could not have two husbands because then noone would know the child's father. Therefore, the apparently more lenient stance of the adultery commandment for men fit the times and did not give him additional freedom because he was allowed many wives.

Our society today is much different. A man is not allowed to have more than 1 wife at a time multiple wives and women are not considered property but, rather, people in their own right. Under these conditions it makes more sense to equalized the adultery law so that both partners in a marriage agree that they will not engage in sexual relationships outside of the marriage. This agreement is based on respect for each other, a commitment to the equality of each partner, and the knowledge that extra-marital sexual relationships tend to be damaging to a marriage.

8. You shall not steal.

On the surface, this commandment seems strait forward and we can feel confident that we don't take things that belong to someone else; or do we? Do we pay our employees generously, or do we pay as little as we can get by with? Do we present someone else's ideas as our own and fail to acknowledge the source? Do we charge what the traffic will bear rather than a fair price? In each of these actions we steal what rightfully belongs to someone else.

In modern Hebrew ⊐.⅃.⅄ means to steal; however, some scholars think that in biblical times   meant to steal a person--usually to sell as a slave. Even if this were true, the theft of property is prohibited in Leviticus.

9. You shall not answer your fellow person with false
testimony.

This commandment exhorts us not to shade or distort or

embellish or deny the truth. In short, lying is not kosher

because false testimony could seriouly damage another

person. False testimony could also damage the person doing

the lying. Remember the story of the boy who called wolf.

He cried for help when there was no wolf and when a wolf

finally came, noone came to help him. Surely the Dotson case

is a good example of the harm that can be done when someone

gives false testimony. Noone knows whether Ms. Webb lied

when she accused Dotson of rape or when she declared him to

be innocent. Dotson has been in jail 6 years, whether justly

or unjustly we don't know. The woman has been publically

discredited and perhaps has made it more difficult to

prosecute a rapist which certainly harms a great many women.

10. You shall not desire your neighbor's house. You shall
not desire your neighbor's wife nor his manservant nor his
maidservant nor his ox nor his ass or anything that your
neighbor has.

Basically, this commandmant warns us about wanting

something that someone else has. Very often, it is this very

strong desire to have what another person has, that causes us

to lie, steal, commit adultery, or even to murder. While it

may not be possible to never experience the emotion of

coveting, it is possible to control our behavior so that we

do not act on this strong emotion.

In the section of Mishna called   קִדּוּשִׁין אֶשֶׁת

the Ethics of the Fathers, Ben Zoma says: Who is rich? The one who takes pleasure in his/her portion." Or, in modern vernacular, the one who is happy with what s/he has. This statement is the positive side of the commandment not to covet.

I want to say something about the hebrew word רֵעַ ,which I translated as fellow person in the ninth commandment and as neighbor in the tenth commandment. In BDB this word is defined as friend, companion, or fellow person. One could ask whether these commandments are talking about how we should treat our friends or anyone in general. During the first millenium B.C.E. רֵעַ probably meant the friends or companions with whom one travelled in a semi-nomadic life style. Today with satalites, television, and jet planes we are more aware of people throughout the world. Therefore, today רֵעַ probably should mean fellow person.

There is a midrash which helps explain why we should follow the mitzvot. "R. Simeon b. Yohai taught: I am God to all the inhabitants of the world, but I have associated My Name only with My people Israel. I am not called the God of the nations, (I am called) the God of Israel." Because God has associated his/her/its name with בְּנֵי יִשְׂרָאֵל, the children of Israel, namely, us; we are responsible for keeping God's mitzvot.

אֲנִי בַּת מִצְוֹת הַיּוֹם

Today, I am a daughter of the commandments. It is with great joy that I make a public declaration of what has slowly occured in my life--the acceptance of the yoke of the mitzvot. I do this out of love of God and a belief that a return to God and living according to God's laws is the only way for humanity to avoid self-destruction.

STANDING AT SINAI

During the spring of 2020, everything was shut down because of the Covid 19 pandemic. We could not attend services in shul so we had to *daven* (pray) at home. When I was davening on Saturday, May 2, 2020, an image popped into my head of me standing at Mt. Sinai. The sky was cloudy yet full of light. This image was so vivid that I actually felt I was standing at Sinai. I could not get the image out of my head, but I could not draw it because it was the Sabbath. So, the next day I tried drawing the image that I saw. I was pleased with the drawing because it got the image out of my head. I had used water-soluble colored pencils; when I added water to the drawing many of the details were lost. On Monday, I showed it to my art teacher who helped me make it better. The more I followed her suggestions the better it got. Finally, I finished the picture 10 days after I had started it.

The following *Shabbat* two lines of poetry popped into my head. Because it was *Shabbat,* I could not write them down. It was a few days before the entire poem jelled and I wrote

it down. The poem and the picture complement each other extremely well. I submitted them for the *Shavuot* booklet that our congregation published in lieu of gathering together for study and prayer on *Shavuot*.

STANDING AT SINAI

Standing at Sinai I see Moses silhouetted against the sky.

A sky like none I have ever seen before.

Full of light and swirling clouds,
    low rumbles of sound and lightning.
        Sights and sounds rather frightening—even the
            unmistakable sound of the shofar.

And then, silence!
Suddenly, words started pouring into me
        beginning with

אנכי

The Hebrew word in bold type is pronounced *"a-no-chee"* and means "I AM" in English; it is the first word that G1d utters when giving the Ten Commandments.[13]

---

13 Different Christian denominations begin counting the decalogue in different places and number the commandments differently.

4

Being a *Malach*

TWICE IN MY LIFE I have had the opportunity to be *a malach*,[14] a messenger from Gld. The first time was a really odd occurrence involving several visionary experiences. The first experience occurred in 1985. In that vision, I was standing before Gld and the hosts of heaven (the heavenly army). There was a man in a chariot who was beside me and called me sister. In front of me was a black amorphous form. The man in the chariot zapped the black form with something like a lightening bolt until it was no more. I did not know what this vision meant.

Then I had another vision of a group of men sitting around an oval table. I was shown that all of the men, except one, were righteous. I was not familiar with any of these men. I was instructed to give this message to GS, a presbyterian minister who lived a few houses away from me. In return for giving GS the message "that one man was not righteous", he would explain the meaning of the other vision to *me*. I felt really silly and uncomfortable going to his house to give him the message. Nonetheless and not without some hesitation, I did knock on his door and described the visions to him. He

---

14 *Malach* means messenger or angel in Hebrew.

explained the first vision by saying that G1d wanted something out of my life and I had to figure out what it was. As for the second vision, I told him that G1d wanted me to give him the message that there was an unrighteous individual in a group of men with whom he was dealing.

In thinking about what G1d wanted out of my life, I came to understand that I had made a false god out of my therapist. I understood that I needed to get out of that relationship and I did so.

Not too long after I gave the message to GS, a fellow clergyman and member of his church's governing board brought charges of heresy against GS. The heresy fight lasted all summer. In the end, the minister who brought the charges did not show up for the last phase of the proceedings, so, the charges against GS were dropped and GS was cleared of heresy. The message from G1d was a warning that there was a snake in the grass among the men with whom he dealt.

▪ ▪ ▪

The second time that I was a *malach* was during the summer of 2011. My husband and I had been invited to have lunch with an older Brazilian couple from our synagogue after *Shabbat* services. The woman left before the service was over so she could make sure that everything was ready for *shabbat* lunch. We accompanied her husband to their home after *Kiddush*[15] at the synagogue was over. The day was sunny,

---

15 *Kiddush* is a time of food and wine/grape juice and chatting after the morning service is over. The word *kiddush* refers to the blessing said over the wine/grape juice. It comes from the Hebrew word meaning to make holy.

hot and humid—a typical summer day in St. Louis. The couple lived about a mile from the synagogue. As we walked, we began moving more and more slowly. The man began feeling faint and needed to rest frequently, either sitting on a stone wall in the sun or leaning against a tree in the shade. My husband and I walked on either side of the man supporting him by holding his elbows and helping him maintain his balance. The situation was especially frightening because we did not know where he lived; because it was *Shabbat*, we were not carrying phones so we could not call his wife for help. It took us an hour to cover a distance normally covered in 20 minutes. In this case, there was no message from G1d, nothing supernatural, but if we had not been with the man, he would have collapsed on his way home. My husband and I really felt like *malachim*, messengers.

5

Soul Vibrations

IN THE SUMMER OF 2000, my husband and I had the opportunity to study in Jerusalem at the rabbinical school for Reform Judaism under the auspices of the Liberal Yeshiva. The setting was ideal, and the two weeks spent there were very satisfying. An odd experience occurred on the way up to Jerusalem from the airport. We were in the mountains leading up to Jerusalem when I was suddenly aware of an awful banging inside my chest [no, it wasn't my heart beating fast]. It felt like something trying to get out by banging against concrete walls, only the walls were my physical body. It was quite uncomfortable, but I sensed that my soul wanted to escape my body and go to the top of the hill we were passing. I could not see anything but sensed that it was either a place or companion soul to which my soul yearned to go. After a few minutes, the banging stopped and everything inside me went back to normal.

While we were in Jerusalem, one of my husband's colleagues invited us to spend *Shabbat* with him in *Kiryat Shmuel. Kiryat Shmuel* is a small, modern orthodox community just north of Haifa. During *Shabbat* all of the roads entering and leaving *Kiryat Shmuel* were blocked which means there were no cars, trains or buses going in or around the town. The town was quiet and an atmosphere of spirituality pervaded it. Inside the home no one used phones or computers and the lights were on timers. Therefore, in *Kiryat Shmuel* there was *Shabbat* outside the house as well as inside the house. When it was time to light candles to bring in *Shabbat*, the community alarm sounded so everyone lit at the correct time. Then all of the men and some of the women walked to synagogue and an atmosphere of peace descended on the community. It was an amazing experience!

The weekend in *Kiryat Shmuel* changed my life. First, I realized that following the commandments of orthodox Judaism led to the formation of a spiritual community. It was not just doing rituals by rote. G1d played a central role in the community. When we got back home, we began going to a conservative synagogue; we started keeping kosher, we no longer drove a car or used electricity on *Shabbat*, in short, we became observant Jews.

Being in *Kiryat Shmuel* resonates with my soul and it is where my soul is happiest. Eventually we bought an apartment in *Kiryat Shmuel* that we used in the winter when my husband was collaborating with Israeli scientists. It was in *Kiryat Shmuel* that I began writing about my spiritual experiences and doing art work inspired by prayers and Torah.

▪ ▪ ▪

Another time that I was physically aware of my soul inside me was when I was reading the last chapter of *Emissary of*

Light by James Twyman.[16] When Mr. Twyman described the Door to Eternity and the process of going through the door, I was aware of a vibration, like a noiseless hum, occurring inside of me. It seemed to me that my soul felt a resonance with the words I was reading; I sensed a truth, and I wanted to go through the door.

▪ ▪ ▪

I used to go to synagogue every Saturday morning, however, when lockdowns started during March 2020 because of the Covid 19 pandemic, I started praying at home. I noticed that if I skimmed the Hebrew words of a prayer at "just the right speed" I could feel a resonance inside me that let me know my soul was happy. If I went too fast or too slow, there would be no resonance from my soul. I have grown so accustomed to this resonance from my soul that now I prefer to pray at home rather than attend synagogue services.

---

16   Twyman, James F. *Emissary of Light, Findhorn Press. 2007*

6

Tsfat[17]

IN MAY OF 1997, I accompanied my husband to Israel for a scientific meeting. We decided to go a week before the meeting because I wanted to visit *Tsfat*. In the sixteenth century a number of great rabbis congregated in *Tsfat*, which became a center of mystical learning. I wanted to visit *Tsfat* to figure out why so many great rabbis lived there. Also, I wondered whether my grandmother's second husband was a descendent of Rabbi Isaac Luria, the great kabbalist. The reason I wondered about this was three-fold: first, his last name was Lurie, second he was a very religious man who taught me a lot about Judaism, and third, his Hebrew name was *"Ari."* Rabbi Luria was also called the *"Ari"*[18] which is short for *"Elohi Rabbi Itzhak"* – the Godly Rabbi Isaac.

We rented a car at the airport, drove to Tsfat and eventually found the Ruth Rimon, where we had a reservation for three days. Our hotel room was facing west toward Mt. Meron; we were on the ground floor with a patio facing a lovely garden. When we went to the dining room for dinner,

---

17   Tsfat is a town in the upper Galilee and is also known as Safed.

18   In Hebrew, the word *"ari"* means lion

we were surprised by the huge number of guests. Evidently, this hotel was a regular stop for tour buses.

Our first afternoon in *Tsfat* we explored the ancient city— visiting synagogues and shops. The next day we went to the old cemetery to look for the graves of some of the famous rabbis. In 1997, the cemetery was mostly loose, sandy gravel. We made our way to the grave of Rabbi Luria. There was a candle lit and people were crying and praying over the grave. One woman had actually draped herself over the grave. I felt absolutely nothing so we made our way to the grave of Rabbi Joseph Karo.[19] As we were walking, my left foot caught on a rock and my right foot slid out from under me. At first, I could not straighten my left leg but once I got it straight, I thought everything was all right. We decided to walk the mile back to our hotel. I could barely walk, but leaning heavily on my husband, we made it. Once again, the dining room was filled with people.

The next day I could hardly walk, so my husband insisted on taking me to the hospital. It turned out that I had broken my fibula near the knee and had sprained my ankle. After the doctor put my leg in a cast, we returned to our hotel. All I could do was sit on our patio, enjoy the beautiful garden and look at Mt. Meron. Meanwhile, my husband wandered the streets of *Tsfat* trying to buy crutches for me; he had no luck because the hospital rented crutches, so there was no need to sell them. Unfortunately, the hospital only rented crutches to Israelis. He did come back with two unmatched canes. When we went to dinner, the dining room was empty and

---

19 Joseph Karo is the author of the *Shulchan Aruch* which is a compilation of Jewish laws *(halacha)* derived from the Talmud.

quiet. We were able to sit by the window and watch the sun go down behind Mt. Meron. The pale pastel colors of the sky were lovely, nothing dramatic, it was then I saw the golden sparkles that I associate with the fifth dimension, the spiritual dimension. Now, I knew why these rabbis had congregated in *Tsfat* and why they would go out into the fields to welcome *Shabbat*. It took several days of sitting quietly before I could see the spiritual dimension around *Tsfat* and understand why the great mystical rabbis had gathered there. My question had been answered but it took a broken leg to enforce the necessity of being quiet. [Therefore, be careful what you ask for.] Because I broke my leg, I went back to the United States instead of going to the scientific meeting in Jerusalem.

ADDENDUM: FUNNY STORIES
RELATED TO OUR TRIP TO *TSFAT*

DRIVING THROUGH AFULA

The shortest, fastest way from Ben Gurion airport to *Tsfat* was through the Arab town of Afula. As we entered the town, we noticed that all of the street signs were in Arabic, which neither of us could read. There was no straight road through Afula and our map was not very helpful. Wrong turn after wrong turn we finally spotted a tour bus. It seemed reasonable to follow the bus in hopes that it would get us to the other side of town. Our strategy worked and at last we saw Afula in the rear-view mirror.

CONFUSION AT THE HOSPITAL

Once we decided to go to the hospital to check on my leg, we ran into some communication problems. The first problem was an armed guard at the entrance to the parking lot. He spoke no English and my Hebrew was nonexistent. I knew words from the Torah but not many words in modern Hebrew. I could not understand his questions let alone explain why we wanted to go to the hospital. Finally, I pointed to my leg and said "*shever*"[20] several times and the guard let us pass.

Once we entered the hospital, we went to the registration desk and explained our problem. I was immediately asked for my visa. I thought they were asking for my visa to be in Israel. I explained that I was American and did not need a visa to be in Israel. This back and forth about "visa" went on for a few minutes until one of the secretaries pulled out a visa credit card.[21] What they really wanted was a credit card so they would be assured of being paid.

Once the diagnosis had been made and a cast put on my leg, we came to the next problem—crutches. The cast on my leg was not a walking cast so I needed some help getting around. This hospital only loaned crutches to Israelis and did not sell them. My husband spent the rest of the day trying to buy crutches in *Tsfat* while I sat on our patio enjoying the garden and Mt. Meron. However, none of the stores sold crutches because people could borrow them from the hospital. In desperation, he bought 2 mismatched canes. The next morning, he went back to the hospital to try and buy crutches. He offered 5 times the price of a pair of crutches but they still would not budge—crutches were only available for loan to Israelis.

---

20 *Shever* is the transliteration of the Hebrew word, שבר which means "break."

21 I use a MasterCard

7

Fusion of Body and Soul

ON FEBRUARY 1, 2012, as I was reading these words:[22] "God has given each of us a purpose in life—to commit and encourage acts of goodness, to use our time, energy, and knowledge to tear through the layers of the 'container' and reveal God's light within." I became aware of a resonance within, not unlike the resonance that accompanied reading about the eternal door in *Emissary of Light*.[23] However, this time the resonance was NOT trapped within my physical body like it was on the way to Jerusalem; instead, there was resonance through out my body and soul. At that moment I understood that my body and soul had fused together. My soul was able to extend through the body even while remaining grounded within the body. This fusion of body and soul brings a sense of peace and joy that is not usually experienced. There was no talking in my brain, just harmony. The trick is to maintain this fusion when one is confronted with the stress of everyday living. I have not yet achieved this state permanently.

---

22 Jacobson, Simon. *Toward a Meaningful Life*, Harper-Collins Publishers. 2002 p278.

23 Twyman, James F. *Emissary of Light*, Findhorn Press. 2007. I described this experience in more detail on page 39.

I do not believe that I am exceptional; therefore, everyone has the capacity to experience their soul, that piece of G1d inside them. What is the secret of experiencing our soul and connecting to G1d? First, we must open ourselves by removing our thoughts, our emotions and our desires. When we open ourselves, we minimize our egos and allow space for our soul to shine. Prayer, meditation and deeds of compassion also help us discover our soul and enable it to mature so that it can master the ego.

A good analogy for opening ourselves is blowing out the insides of an egg so that one can decorate the eggshell. There must be two holes—one to blow into and the other to allow the egg white and the yolk to pass through.   Blowing out an egg is similar to clearing our mind of thoughts, desires and emotions. When we open ourselves, we come into contact with our spiritual core. This contact allows the divine energy to pass through us and into the world. Every time we do deeds of compassion or acts of kindness, we allow the divine energy to flow into the world.

I drew this picture to illustrate the fusion of my soul with my body.

▪ ▪ ▪

On August 22, 2020, as I was praying the morning prayers for *Shabbat,* I noticed a feeling of anxiety in my stomach. This was unusual for me because I normally feel the happiness of my soul as I pray these words. I stopped saying the prayer and asked G1d to explain the problem. The following image appeared in my head. I drew a sketch of it the next day and painted it later in the week. My soul is the white object surrounded by yellow. The yellow represents the spiritual dimension. Notice the rays, they represent my soul's connection to everything. The darker areas in the corners represent objects in the material world as seen through the spiritual

dimension. I think my anxiety came from the feeling that my soul was on a journey. It was still connected to me but not in the same way as before.

Some months later another image came into my head. This time my soul was connecting to a group of souls. Notice that my soul is still connected to me via a thin extension which is represented by the white line extending from my soul as it

is fusing with this group of souls. I assume that this group of souls is my soul pod.

The picture below shows a pod of souls within the spiritual dimension.

8

The Tree

SOMETIME DURING THE SUMMER of 2010, I had a very odd experience. Every evening I took a two-mile walk for exercise and to maintain a healthy blood glucose level. One evening as I was returning home, I suddenly became aware of a profound feeling of sadness. I took another step or two before I turned around to see if I could identify the source of the sadness. There were no people or animals around; the source of the incredible sadness seemed to be coming from a tree that I had just passed. The tree looked fine, it had no marks or tape and it did not appear to be ill. Nonetheless, there was pervasive sadness radiating from the tree. I walked over to the tree and was so overwhelmed by the sadness coming from it that I put my arms around the tree in an effort to comfort it. After a short while, I continued on my way home thinking how bizarre it was to feel sadness from a tree.

Two days later when I came upon the tree that had emitted such sadness, I was shocked by what I saw—all of the branches of the tree had been sawed off and only the trunk remained. The trunk was about 10 feet tall and the truncated branches extended not more than a foot from the tree. I felt incredible sadness for the tree and from the tree. Again, I hugged the tree and told it that I hoped it could recover from the butchering it had received. Within a week, the rest of the tree was gone and the trunk was pulverized into the ground. When the trunk was gone there was no more sadness in that area (except for my own at the loss of the tree).

Needless to say, I had and still have many questions about this odd experience. How could the tree know it was going to be cut down? How could the tree feel and express its emotions? How could I sense the tree's distress? What made me sensitive to this particular tree?

When an Israeli friend of ours heard my story about the tree, he showed me a dead palm tree in his neighbor's yard. The palm tree had been planted 30 years earlier by his neighbor. The neighbor cared for the tree and the tree grew. In September 2012, the neighbor died and by January 2013, the palm tree was dead. How did the palm know that the man who had cared for it had died? What was the connection between the palm tree and the man?

At the burning bush[24] when G1d asked Moses to travel to Pharaoh in Egypt to free the Israelite slaves, Moses gave five reasons that he should not go. One of the reasons was that he did not know G1d's name. In response to being asked His name, G1d answered:[25] "*Ehyeh asher ehyeh*" which means "I will be what I will be." Some people translate this phrase as "I am that I am"; however, there is no present tense of the verb "to be" in Hebrew. If one thinks about these translations, "I will be what I will be" implies change whereas "I am that I am" is static. Before my experience with the tree, I interpreted the phrase "*Ehyeh asher ehyeh*" to mean that G1d would appear

---

24 Exodus Chapter 3

25 Ex 3:14

to a person in a way that the person needed. This situation would lead to different views of G1d. Therefore, we would have different religions and ways of relating to G1d.

After my experience with the tree, it occurred to me that the phrase might mean something more extensive. It could suggest that G1d experiences the universe by being part of its various animate and inanimate objects. I cannot fathom that much simultaneous input!

Most people believe we have a soul—a part of G1d that is inside each of us; but couldn't G1d also be a part of trees or rocks. Did this tree have a part of G1d within it that was able to communicate with the part of G1d in me? If this supposition were true, then everything would be interconnected and the appearance of separateness would be an illusion. The book *Sefer Yetzirah*,[26] an early mystical work, suggests there is such a dimension. This dimension is in addition to the dimensions of space and time and can be considered a fifth dimension. I think of it as the spiritual dimension.

---

26 Aryeh Kaplan, *Sefer Yetzirah The book of Creation: in theory and practice*; Samuel Weiser, Inc. 1993

לך לאמונה
לך לכבוד יה
לך לדעת השם
לך לשלום לך לך

B.Templeton

9

Night Time Poem

ONE NIGHT IN 2014, when I was in *Kiryat Shmuel* Israel, I awoke at 2:30 in the morning with the words of a Hebrew poem in my head. I got up and wrote down the words so I would not forget them. They seemed like a message to me from Gld. As I looked at the words in the morning and thought about them during the day, I felt that they were telling me to pursue my artistic ideas even though doing art frightened me because I do not consider myself an artist. Somehow, these words mitigated my fear and enabled me to begin and continue projects that I had been thinking about.

Here are the words of the poem and an English translation.

Go to/for faith	לך לאמונה
Go to/for the honor of Yah (*HaShem*)	לך לכבוד יה
Go to/for knowledge of *HaShem*[27]	לך לדעת השם
Go to/for peace,[28] Go to/for yourself or Go! Go!	לך לשלום לך לך

---

27 *HaShem* refers to Gld's formal name; literally it means "the name"
28 I translated the Hebrew word *Shalom* as peace, but it can also mean completeness.

When a ל is attached to the beginning of a word, it can mean "to" or "for", therefore I used both words in the English translation. It is for you, the reader, to decide which translation you prefer. The Hebrew word לך without vowels can be either the imperative tense of the English word "go" OR it can mean "to you or for you." At the beginning of each line לך means "go." The Hebrew word לך appears twice at the end of the last line; therefore, those two words could mean "go to yourself" or "go for yourself" or "Go! Go!" It is up to you to decide which translation you prefer.

In Genesis 12:1, G1d called Abraham with these same two words לך לך. G1d told Abraham to leave his current surroundings and go to an unknown place. This is a scary proposition. Perhaps, Abraham also heard the words of this poem and they enabled him to leave all that he knew and head for the unknown.

Eventually, I turned this poem into a piece of art that hangs over my desk. The words of the poem are arranged like a staircase extending from heaven to earth. The use of a staircase is to remind the viewer of Gen 28:12 in which Jacob dreams of a *sulam,* a staircase,[29] extending from earth to heaven. I arranged the poem in this form to show that there is always a connection to G1d even when we do not know it.

---

29 This word is also translated as ladder.

10

Recent Experiences

THE ROSE

WHILE I WAS DAVENING the *Shabbat* prayers on June 6, 2020, a beautiful image came into my head. The image was of a golden rose rooted in the "hand" of G1d; the rose had 13 petals. I had to wait until after Shabbat before I could draw what I had seen. The picture below shows the image that I saw.

I wondered what the image meant. I knew that the Zohar[30] began with a description of a 13 petaled rose that is red and white. This rose is likened to the congregation of Israel. According to the Zohar, each petal alludes to one of G1d's 13 attributes of mercy[31] that surround the rose to protect it. I have often viewed the 13 petals as the 11 full tribes of Israel plus the two half-tribes of Ephraim and Menashe. This idea is

---

30   Zohar 1:1. The Zohar is the "Book of Splendor" which interprets the Hebrew Bible in a mystical way. The *Zohar* is written in Aramaic and is difficult. An accessible translation was done by Daniel C. Mott; another translation was done by Michael Laitman. Both translations have copious notes but the book by Laitman goes much more deeply into *Kabbala*, the literature of Jewish mysticism.

31   Exodus 34:6-7

supported by the "concluding section"[32] of a medieval poem that is chanted after the book of Esther is read on *Purim*.[33] This section begins with the words: "*shoshanat yaacov*" which means "the rose of Jacob" and refers to all Jews living in Persia.

For a long time, I interpreted my vision as showing that the assembly of Israel was rooted in G1d. After a while I began to wonder about this interpretation because the rose in the Zohar was red and white but I had seen a golden rose. It occurred to me that the golden rose might represent me being grounded in G1d. I have always viewed myself as a yellow rose for two reasons: 1) I had blond hair in my youth and to this day it is blond in the sun or bright lights; 2)my maiden name was Rosenblatt, which means rose leaf/petal in German. My first name means "pretty" so I viewed myself as a pretty rose petal, a golden one of course.

UR KASDIM

On *Shabbat*, October 30, 2021, as I was praying, I had an interesting experience. The phrase אור כשדים (*Ur Kasdim*) in one of the prayers[34] jumped out at me and began mutating in my head. This phrase refers to the land surrounding and in between the Tigris and Euphrates rivers, modern day Iraq. In the Bible, Abraham comes from *Ur Kasdim*.[35] The following list shows how the phrase in the prayer mutated in my head into a different meaning.

---

32 *Siddur Sim Shalom for Shabbat and Festivals.* The rabbinical Assembly 1998 p220

33 Purim celebrates the deliverance of the Jews from destruction.

34 *Vay'varech David*

35 Gen 11:28, 31; 15:7

מְאוּר כַּשְׂדִּים

מאור כשדים

מאור כשדים

מאור כשדים

אוֹר שַׁדַּי

The first line is the phrase as it is found in the prayer that I
was reading. It means "from *Ur Kasdim.*" In the second line,
I have removed the vowels; the handwritten *Torah* has no
vowels or punctuation. The third line highlights the letters
to which I want to draw attention. In the fourth line, I have
minimized the unimportant letters and now, in the fifth line,
we have the phrase, "*Or Shaddai,*" which means "light of
Shaddai."

The Hebrew word *Shaddai* is one of the names of G1d in
the *Torah.* In the *Torah*, it is frequently used with the word
El which means G1d.[36] In the *Mishna*[37] there is a discussion

---

36 Gen 35:11; Ex 6:2

37 The *Mishna* is an early collection of oral commentaries on Jewish law.

of the names of G1d that cannot be erased; *Shaddai* (used without *El*) is one of G1d's names that cannot be erased.[38]

Thus, we have gone from the name of a place (*Ur Kasdim*) to the light of *Shaddai*. Who is the light of *Shaddai*? Our forefather *Avram* left *Ur Kasdim* and became *Avraham*, the light of *Shaddai*—the light of G1d. In the Middle East it was *Avraham* who brought the light of G1d into the world. In the modern world, each of us has the opportunity to bring the light of G1d into the world.

I consider the insight to see this word mutation a gift from G1d.

COINCIDENCES

Coincidences happen to everyone. The issue becomes, does one see these coincidences as signs from G1d or happening by chance alone. The answer to this question lies in the eyes of the person who experiences them. The following set of coincidences happened to me between July of 2021 and February of 2022.

In mid-July, I began to have pain in the mouth/sinus area on the left side of my face. There was nothing unusual about this because when I had a sinus infection, it often felt like a toothache. I did go to urgent care and got Augmentin, the normal antibiotic for sinus infections. It did not work as well as normal, so I went to see my dentist. She thought I had a tooth infection and sent me to an endodontist for a root canal. The endodontist thought I had a large cyst and sent me to an oral surgeon, and I was scheduled for surgery two weeks

---

38 Shavuot 35a 27

later. All of this time, I was on a variety of antibiotics.[39] The timeframe for these appointments took me into the Hebrew month of *Elul* which is the time of preparation for the Jewish new year and the Day of Atonement.

I take this time of preparation seriously and examine my behavior through the past year and choose an area of behavior that I would like to improve. This year because I had a lot of pain in my mouth, I asked myself if G1d was sending me a message about my mouth. I realized that I had gotten into the habit of speaking ill about rabbis and congregations. So, I decided to work on *Lashon Hara*. Literally *Lashon Hara* means "evil speech." The first two times I heard evil speech I felt my jaws clamped together. I had not done the clamping, it had been done for me. I got the idea and thanked G1d for the help. After that I was on my own to not speak *Lashon Hara*. This task is not so easy because we love talking about each other. When the situation of *Lashon Hara* came up, I would say: "I was working on *Lashon Hara* so I could not participate in the conversation." I made this comment in front of a Chabad rabbi who said that what I had said still had the "dust of *Lashon Hara*" attached to it. After this comment, I did not know what to say.

In February 2022, the rabbi of my congregation called and asked if I would be willing to participate in a program called "clean speech." This program was taking place in various cities through-out the United States. The goal of the program was

---

39   My dental problems continued even after the oral surgery and the root canal. The infection kept recuring and eventually my tooth was removed 4 December 2021 and I took even more antibiotics. Hopefully the infection has been cured.

to help people become aware of the words that come out of their mouths and try to effect change to more positive speech. I agreed to participate as long as there was not too much work involved. I was afraid that I would have to study and write an essay. It turned out that all I had to do was show up and read an essay from a teleprompter. I was sent a copy of my reading a week before the filming. The reading that I was assigned had the **perfect response** for when one finds oneself in a situation where *Lashon Hara* arises: "I am working to keep what I hear and speak positive, so could we change the topic of this conversation." This way no one would be chastised for speaking *Lashon Hara*. The reading that I was assigned was so perfect for me that I felt was a gift from G1d.

The last coincidence related to participating in the "clean speech" program happened on the day of the filming. For some reason, I took the wrong route on my way to the filming appointment. Once I figured out how to fix my mistake, I did get to the location on time but much later than I had anticipated. I arrived at the door at the same time as another woman who had just realized that she had forgotten her key. I had a phone number to call so the woman did not have to go back home for her key. Had I not gone the wrong way, I would not have been there to help the woman enter the building.

It is through coincidences that one can **look back** and see G1d's hand in one's life. It was not until I told this story to someone that I realized this series of coincidences was laid out by G1d.

11

Mystical Experiences of Other People

MY MOTHER DIED IN October of 1977. I was not in the hospital room with her but my brothers told me that her last words, before she slipped into a coma, were "Oh G1d." I have always wondered what she saw.

On the day of her funeral, my maternal grandmother told us a story that happened a day or two before her husband, my maternal grandfather, died in 1951. She said she came into his room and saw him wrapped in a glowing, golden light. A while after that she said he asked for his *tefillin* and prayer shawl.[40] These ritual objects were brought to him and he put them on. Clearly, he had had a profound mystical experience just before he died.

■ ■ ■

I know several people who have had mystical experiences in their lives. Their experiences were different than mine and I wanted to offer the reader a variety of examples of mystical experiences. Two of my friends agreed to write about their experiences. These people are identified by their initials.

---

40   These are Jewish ritual objects that are worn by Jewish men during prayer.

MYSTICAL EXPERIENCES OF AES

SAVED BY A BUS

When I was around 15 years old, my church youth group rented a bus to drive us to Denver to see one of the big epic films. It could have been *Ben Hur*, or *The Ten Commandments*. Our parents were told to pick us up in front of the Aggie Theater on College Avenue at a certain time. It was late, almost midnight, when we arrived at the theater, and all the other parents were there. Everyone assumed that my parents were there, and they all drove off, leaving me standing alone. There was no traffic and no pedestrians anywhere.

Suddenly, a man drove by slowly and stared at me. He drove around the block and returned, then parked on the opposite side of the street. He began walking slowly and deliberately toward me, and I was terrified. He looked like a predator stalking his prey, and I knew instinctively that he intended to harm me. I had never seen such a look of pure evil before. There was no one to help me, and no place I could hide. Screaming wouldn't have brought any rescue. I had forgotten that there was a small hotel at the other end of the block, but it was on the opposite side of the street and impossible to reach in time.

Just as the man came to the middle of the wide street, a big Greyhound bus pulled up next to me, blocking the man's progress. An elderly woman stepped out of the bus, looked directly at me, and said, "Will you please help me carry my suitcase to the hotel?" I rushed to pick up her suitcase, the bus pulled away, and the man stared in disbelief as we crossed the street only yards from him. It was clear that he was shocked and angry that I had gotten away.

I called my parents from the safety of the hotel and flagged them down when I saw them. As we pulled away from the curb, I saw the man drive by again, and I told my parents about my narrow escape. He clearly was hoping that he would have another chance with me. I don't think my parents realized the extreme danger I had been in.

Looking back on this I know that I was in the presence of pure evil, I have always felt that an angel interceded in the form of that woman. The timing of the bus was so extraordinary, I remain convinced that I was saved by some force or entity greater than myself.

CHARTRES CATHEDRAL, OCTOBER 12, 2002

My husband and I took a two-hour train ride to Chartres to visit the cathedral. It was a gloomy, rainy day, with no sun in sight. After lunch in the town, we walked to the cathedral and went inside. It was still dark and cloudy outside as we entered the cathedral. I lit a candle and said a prayer for our children near the entrance. Then we paused to look at the Vierge de Pilier, a black Madonna. I asked the Madonna to watch over our children. We then walked toward the ambulatory and as we approached the first pillar past the Virgin, we suddenly saw a perfect heart shape, projected by a very intense beam of light, on the pillar at eye level. The light appeared to come from an angle above us and on the opposite side of the church. I thought that perhaps it was a light installation produced by an artist because we had seen a similar one earlier in the week at St. Eustache in Paris. But we soon realized that the image was caused by a missing piece of glass in one of the ambulatory's topmost windows. That tiny gap, no bigger than an inch or two in diameter, acted as a lens to produce this extremely

intense beam of light. My husband and I each stood briefly in the light to verify this. The light moved fairly quickly to the right and onto a flat part of the pillar, so that the light became circular. And within that circle appeared the dark and very sharp silhouette of a cross. This was created by the shadow of a sculpted stone cross on the top of the choir.

It was over in two or three minutes, but the experience lingered in my mind. I even tried to take a photo of it, but the flash went off so all I have is an image of the pillar. Perhaps I was not supposed to take a photo. What an uncanny coincidence, that just the two of us were there at the exact time this occurred. The light was extraordinarily bright, intense. The way that it moved and slightly quivered made it seem alive.

It radiated peace and joy and made me feel very happy. I felt as if it were telling me that 'everything is going to be all right'.

It was uncanny how sunlight, sculpture and pillar aligned perfectly to create this remarkable image. It was a natural phenomenon, but it also was an extraordinary coincidence, and I can't help but believe that it was also a great gift intended solely for us. I wondered how the sunlight suddenly broke through at just the right time to show us these images, especially since it had been such a cloudy day. And no one else was around when this happened, which is unusual in such a famous shrine. I will always remember this as one of the spiritual highlights of my life.

DELHI, INDIA JULY 14, 2010

I stayed at our hosts' home today because I had stomach pains and didn't feel well. The day went by very slowly, and I began to think about our son Patrick, who had died in a climbing accident in 2000. I had found a climbers' blog yesterday that talked about Patrick. One of the commentators had posted a stunning photo of Patrick climbing. It made me feel the grief of his loss all over again, and the tears flowed. And as I was lying on the bed thinking of him, I looked out the window and saw an eagle land on a big light fixture 15 feet away from my window! I couldn't believe my eyes, and I took several photos of it. I even checked on the internet just to make sure it was an eagle, and it was. The eagle is an important symbol to me because the night after we learned about Patrick's death, I had a dream about a large eagle soaring under the spherical blue ceiling of an enormous building. Because of that dream, we put a phrase from the Bible on his monument: "On eagle's wings." What an uncanny coincidence. I'm still amazed and pondering its significance. I feel like Patrick comes back in bird form to remind me that he is still around.

THE MYSTICAL EXPERIENCES OF ART

MY SPIRITUAL JOURNEY TO JUDAISM

When I was in high school and college, I questioned many things about my Christianity. Unfortunately, my questioning did not lead to answers, only to doubts, and these doubts gradually led to agnosticism, and even atheism. When I was in college, I met my future wife and she was Jewish. At this point, I began going down a novel fork of my spiritual journey.

My wife always had a strong Jewish identity. I admired and respected all that I learned about Judaism from the example of her actions. When we had children, this respect for what I had observed about Judaism made me completely comfortable with raising my children as Jews, but it did not end my own doubts about G1d and religion.

Shortly after our 11th wedding anniversary, while my wife was undergoing surgery, I was sitting alone in the waiting room and my parents were babysitting our two young sons. With no warning, an intense feeling of dread descended upon me, and I feared for her life. Without thinking I began to pray to G1d — praying that she would be allowed to live. As suddenly as this feeling had descended, it lifted and I was calmed. I later found out that my wife had nearly slipped away, not once but twice. My prayer to G1d and my relief for it being answered affirmatively were so automatic that I never thought about the implications. Only later did my wife point out to me that I could no longer regard myself as an atheist or agnostic. As soon as she said this, its truth was self-evident. I then knew two things about Gld, and indeed these still remain the only attributes of Gld that I feel I truly know. I know that Gld exists. I know that Gld cares. This may seem to be very little, but in truth it is a great deal, and I feel blessed to have come to such knowledge.

After my wife's surgery and recovery, our home became much more intensely Jewish. I felt comfortable with this, and helped lead seders, say Sabbath blessings, took great pride in my sons at their *Bar Mitzvah* ceremonies, and I was truly in awe of the spirituality I saw in my wife. The gates to the Law[41] were open to me, but I could not—chose not—to enter. I worshiped Gld in my own personal fashion, feeling Gld's presence most intensely when alone in the forests, mountains, and glades of Gld's creation. I participated in the Jewish life of our household, but always held myself apart from it. I told my wife that although I believed in Gld and worshipped Gld in my own idiosyncratic fashion, I did not find organized religion of any sort meaningful to me. This phase of my spiritual journey lasted nearly two decades, and in hindsight I cannot fully understand why I chose to remain outside Judaism for so long. I had created and empowered some mighty gatekeepers to prevent me from entering the gates: my strong ethnic identity as a Scottish American made it difficult for me to identify as a Jew. I feared the ties of love and respect to my family would be strained by conversion. Also, it was easier to continue as I was rather than to make an active choice of change. I know now that all these gatekeepers were empowered solely by my own fears, doubts, and inertia;

---

41 This phrase has a double meaning. First, it refers to a short story by Kafka and second, the Law can also refer to *Torah*.

and when I finally decided to commit to Judaism, my gate-keepers all dissolved into nothingness.

The decision to become Jewish was made in a distant place—a Zen garden in Japan. In April of 1999, I was invited to attend a scientific conference in Kyoto, the old imperial capital of Japan. The Japanese organizers of this conference had one and only one thing in mind when they set the dates: the conference was to coincide with the height of the cherry blossom season in Kyoto, a city filled with cherry trees and temples. Unfortunately, this meant that we would have to leave for Japan the day before Passover began. The first day of Passover would then disappear as we crossed the International Date Line, and we would arrive on the second day of Passover. The meeting would continue throughout the rest of Passover (covering both Good Friday and Easter as well for the Christians); it was obvious that it would be impossible to keep Passover in Japan. Because of this, my wife decided not to come with me, much to my disappointment. But I was like the second child in the Passover Haggada: Passover was for *you*, not *me*, so *I* could go to Japan even though my wife felt compelled to stay home. Because everyone was jet-lagged, our first day in Kyoto (the second day of Passover) was simply a tourist day. We were led around by our Japanese hosts to see some of the sights of this ancient and beautiful city. Surprisingly, I found myself actively missing Passover. My wife and I had been together 29 years at this time, and this was the first Passover that I was not celebrating with her. I learned in Japan that Passover was for *me* after all.

This is not to imply that I was not enjoying my tour of Kyoto temples, palaces and gardens. These places are beautiful at any time of the year, but with the added beauty of the

cherry blossoms, they were truly spectacular. In the afternoon we visited Ryoanji Temple, a complex of temples, gardens and ponds. Within this complex we came upon a small 15th century zen garden, consisting of only raked white sand and 15 rocks. The pull of this garden upon my soul was strong and immediate; I was totally captivated by its simplicity and beauty. Most of our group looked at this small, plain garden and went on to look at other parts of the temple, but I stayed, mesmerized by the garden. My Japanese host and one of his graduate students came and sat next to me. Professor K. told me that of all the 1700 temples in Kyoto, this garden was his favorite and he came here when he needed peace and spiritual nourishment. He said the rest of the group would have to come back this way, so we could stay if we wanted. I told him that I would indeed like to stay. Professor K.'s student then told me that 15 is a perfect number in Zen Buddhism, but that Soami, the master painter and gardener, had laid out this garden so that you could never see all 15 stones at once. My scientific side rose to ascendancy, and I began walking around the garden. I quickly determined that it did indeed have 15 stones, but that the most you could see from any given angle was 13. Perfection is before our eyes, but we can only see it imperfectly. I finally found a position that let me glimpse perfection in a manner that brought peace and fulfillment to me, even though I knew my glimpse was imperfect and incomplete. Many other people were at the garden, and each one gravitated to a spot that brought them closest to this view of perfection, but that spot differed from person to person. All of us were looking at the same rocks of perfection, this altar of unhewn stones, but we all saw different rocks or different sides of the same rocks.

The rest of the group now returned and, reluctantly, I had to leave the garden. A sense of peace and a heightened appreciation of the great beauty of this temple complex accompanied me as I walked by more gardens and ponds. I had no specific thoughts, only an amorphous feeling of contentment and joy of being alive. As we exited the gates of the temple complex and returned to modern Kyoto, these feelings coalesced into a powerful acceptance of my being Jewish. I describe this moment as being one of acceptance of my Judaism even though technically I had not yet converted, nor even initiated the conversion process. But that is how it felt; it was not a decision to *become* Jewish, it was an acceptance that I already *was* Jewish. Now I had to transform that feeling of acceptance into reality by formally converting.

My first thought was to call my wife immediately, but as we walked farther from the gates, suddenly I was startled: What was happening to me? Could this be real! My very own experience of just moments ago now confused me and I could not understand it. Yet the feeling of being Jewish did not go away. I decided to wait until *Shabbat* (2 days) before calling home. If I still felt the same way, I would tell her of my decision. If the feeling went away, so be it. The feeling did not go away; instead, I felt more and more comfortable with it. On Friday evening (at least in Japan), I called my wife with the news. After nearly 30 years of marriage, it is hard to surprise your spouse, but I succeeded with this phone conversation.

Shortly after I returned to St. Louis, my wife and I went to the *Bat Mitzvah* of one her students. I have gone to many, many *Bar* and *Bat Mitzvah* ceremonies but, this one was the first I had experienced feeling that I was a Jew. I was astounded by the difference this change in attitude made, once again reinforcing my decision. After the *Bat Mitzvah*, while standing in the hallway at the Synagogue, my wife pointed out Rabbi G. to me, who was talking to some people farther down the hall. My wife said she was in charge of outreach, and if I was serious about converting, I should go talk to her. Now was the time to transform my feelings into concrete action, and once again I was beset by a twinge of doubt. I asked my wife to introduce me to the rabbi, but she said I could introduce myself and tell her that I wanted to convert. The smile with which Rabbi G. greeted this news is forever etched into my memory, and all doubts were now gone.

Thus, I began my studies with Rabbi G. and I cannot thank her enough for her wisdom, guidance, and support; not only for studying Judaism with her but also for her help and compassion in applying it to my life in times of difficulty. I also want to thank my wife who became my second "rabbi." As I studied, question after question would pop into my head, and my wife was the nearest target. I was often insatiable, and I know that I tried her patience on more than one occasion. However, the more I learned, the more I was in awe of my wife's depth and breadth of her knowledge.

The more I studied and participated in Judaism, the more I knew that the course I began as I left the temple of Ryoanji was indeed the right path for me. I have been continually astounded at how passages in the *Torah* have helped me and they came along at exactly the right moments in my life. The Jewish perspective gives me the closest glimpse of perfection/G1d that I can obtain with my imperfect senses and mind. I thank G1d for setting me upon this path, and allowing me to become a Jew. I truly did not anticipate the intense joy that has filled me upon formally becoming Jewish. Never has a decision felt more right to me than the decision to become Jewish.

While I was studying for conversion, I was contacted by a group of medical researchers at the Technion Medical School in Haifa, Israel. They wanted access to a computer program that I had written to test for associations between diseases and other traits with DNA sequences. I sent them my program. I am a geneticist and not a computer programmer, therefore, although my program worked, it was "buggy" and prone to crashing. After helping the Israelis via e-mail to overcome several such crashes, they finally decided it would be better for me to fly to Israel to get the program working. There was a special lectureship that they could use for this purpose that was available about two weeks before Passover, and we agreed that I would come on that date and then return to the US in time to celebrate Passover with my family.

After studying with Rabbi G. for just under a year, she decided that I was ready for the *Beit Din*.[42] After answering

---

42 Rabbinical court

the questions of the rabbis, I was sent to the *Mikvah*[43] where I immersed in the water three times, said the appropriate blessings and emerged as a Jew. Three days later, I was flying to Israel to collaborate with the scientists at the Technion Medical School. Via email, I told Professor KS, the head of that group, that I had just converted to Judaism. Although I had been to Israel before for various scientific meetings and for the *Bar Mitzvah* of my younger son, this would be my first trip to Israel as a Jew and I was extremely excited. Professor KS was equally excited by this news. He instructed me to go immediately to Jerusalem and meet a rabbi friend of his who would show me around Jerusalem for several days before proceeding to Haifa.

Upon arriving in Israel, I proceeded directly to a hotel in Jerusalem where I left my luggage. I was extremely excited to be in Israel as a Jew, and everything felt different from my previous trips. My first desire was to walk to the Western Wall to pray. The morning service on Mondays includes reading a portion of the *Torah* section that would be read in full on the next Sabbath, therefore, the Western Wall was quite crowded with many groups for this morning service. As I entered the courtyard in front of the Wall, I saw a group of ultra-orthodox Jews just beginning the morning service. They were dressed in black pants, coats, and hats, while I was dressed in blue jeans with a knitted kipah on my head. (My conversion was a Reform conversion, and some of the Jews at my synagogue had warned me that the ultra-orthodox often look down upon reform Jews, can treat them poorly, and do not recognize Reform conversions.) I knew that I stood out

---

43 Ritual bath

like a sore thumb from the ultra-orthodox men in this group, so I remained at the periphery and tried to make myself as obscure as possible. Finally, the Torah was brought out, and a congregant was called up to bless the Torah before it was read. The Rabbi then began to chant the first portion of the Torah to be read that day. My Hebrew was almost non-existent at this point, so I did not understand a word of what the Rabbi was singing. But I was a Jew, standing in front of the Western Wall, listening to the words of the Torah being sung and joy completely filled me. The first portion ended, and a second man was chosen to come up to say the blessing before the second portion was chanted. As the Rabbi began to sing the second portion, I became aware that the *Gabbai*, the assistant who was in charge of the logistics of the service, was staring intently at me. All the stories of how ultra-orthodox Jews have distain for Reform Jews came back to me and I concluded that I had overstayed my welcome in this group. Therefore, I turned around and began to walk away.

The *Gabbai* immediately ran around the periphery of the group of worshipers and stopped directly in front of me. I was expected a tongue lashing, but instead he said, in English (my dress gave me away), "The final *Aliyah* (coming up to bless the reading of the *Torah)* is for you." I admit that I was in complete shock about his statement; all I could do was stammer "I'm sorry, but my Hebrew is very poor." He answered "That makes no difference. I will help you with the Hebrew. But the next *Aliyah* is definitely for you." So, he led me up front to the *Torah* and helped me bless the *Torah* for the first time. After the *Torah* was read, the *Gabbai* helped me say the appropriate blessing. Once the *Torah* was rolled up and covered, the *Gabbai* gave it to me to hold while the congregants danced around me singing *Aitz Hayim*.[44] I could hardly believe what was happening, and I was filled with the emotions of joy and wonderment as I stood holding a *Torah* at the Western Wall surrounded by singing, dancing Jews.

The service then continued, and when it was over, the *Gabbai* said to me "When I saw you there standing outside our group, *HaShem*[45] told me that the next *Aliyah* was for you. Therefore, I know you have a story to tell me, so tell it!" I briefly recapped my story, ending with my formal conversion on Thursday. At this news, the *Gabbai* smiled broadly and gave me a bear hug, yelling to the Rabbi, "Rabbi, we just *Bar-Mitzvahed* this man!" The Rabbi then came over and also gave me a bear hug, saying "You must come back with me to our home to celebrate your *Bar Mitzvah*." So, I left the Old City with the Rabbi and his followers and went to his home in *Mea She'arim*, an ultra-orthodox neighborhood in Jerusalem.

Once there, I enjoyed a wonderful lunch with the Rabbi, his wife, and many of his students. He ran a *Yeshiva*,[46] and asked me to recount the story of my conversion to his students. The response by all was very positive and supportive, even though, I informed them that my conversion was Reform and that I had studied with a woman Rabbi. After much singing, eating, and discussion of Torah, I finally had to leave in order to keep my appointment with Rabbi B. As I left, the Rabbi gave me another hug and said "I hope you continue your studies of Judaism, and perhaps one day you will study

---

44 *Aitz Hayim* means "a tree of life" which is a metaphor for the *Torah*.

45 *HaShem* literally means "the Name" and refers to G1d's formal name which is not pronounced.

46 A *yeshiva* is a school where Jewish texts are studied.

in my Yeshiva." With that, my *Bar Mitzvah* celebration ended, but my spiritual journey continued more strongly than ever.

Part of this spiritual journey included continuing my work with scientists at the Technion and establishing new collaborations with other Israeli scientists at the University of Haifa and Ben Gurion University. This work brought me back every year from 2000 to 2019 until the Covid pandemic caused a break. I usually spent at least 2-3 months in Israel. I learned on these subsequent stays in Israel that a Reform Jew being given an *Aliyah* by the ultra-orthodox was far from the norm; indeed, most of my Israeli friends could hardly believe that it had happened. However, the *Gabbai* on the day of my *Bar Mitzvah*, had told the Rabbi that *HaShem* had told him that the next *Aliyah* was for me, so of course it had to be. I was not only given the *Aliyah*, but I was treated with great honor and acceptance by this ultra-Orthodox Rabbi and his Yeshiva. In 2002, I had a sabbatical and spent it with my wife in *Kiryat Shmuel*, a modern Orthodox community just north of Haifa where my main collaborator at the Technion lived. I only found out many years later when the Chief Rabbi of *Kiryat Shmuel* died that I had been at a center of controversy. Professor KS had asked this Rabbi for permission to give me an *Aliyah* at the main synagogue. At this point, I had not undergone my second, Halakic conversion to Judaism, and most of the men in the community strongly objected to giving me the honor of an *Aliyah* since the Orthodox do not recognize a Reform conversion. The Rabbi asked KS if he thought I would continue to delve deeper into Judaism and if I would someday buy an apartment in *Kiryat Shmuel* and live there. KS answered yes (and indeed, both turned out to be true). The Rabbi ruled that I should be encouraged in my spiritual journey and that I should receive *Aliyot*.[47] Over the years I received many *Aliyot* in that synagogue even before my second conversion, and I had nothing but honor and support by all the people in the community without a single disparaging word or incident.

---

47 *Alyiot* is the plural of *Alyia.*

12

Concluding Thoughts

THIS BOOK IS A DIARY of my mystical experiences. They occurred sporadically over a period of sixty years and all but one of them occurred spontaneously without any preparation on my part. As a result of these experiences, I have come to understand that there is a fifth dimension in addition to the four that everybody knows (length, width, height, time). I call this dimension the spiritual dimension. Everything, living or not, is connected to this dimension. This connection to the spiritual dimension can be called a spark of G1d or a soul.

I do not believe that I am unique in being able to connect with the spiritual dimension and I have included mystical experiences of other people in Chapter 11 to emphasize this point. From these examples, one can see that people sense the spiritual dimension in different ways. As you have seen in this book, my encounters with G1d have been in the form of dreams or visions. But other people may experience G1d or the spiritual dimension in other ways. For example, many people find it easier to connect with the spiritual dimension when they are alone in nature, whereas, Buddhist monks access the spiritual dimension by meditating. Some people access the spiritual dimension by praying, while others look back at events that have occurred and find coincidences that lead them to see G1d at work in their lives.

The Hebrew scripture[48] suggests that we can see G1d in retrospect. For instance, when Jacob was fleeing from his brother Esau, he dreamt of a ladder extending from earth to heaven with beings ascending and descending on it. When Jacob awoke, he said "*HaShem*[49] is in this place and I did not know" [Gen. 28:16]. We can learn from this story that perhaps G1d has been present in our lives and we did not know it. A person can always look back at his/her life to see if there were odd coincidences or dreams that they could interpret as possible encounters with G1d. We are often unaware of G1d's presence until we have an unusual experience that wakes us up. These unusual experiences are fleeting but they may have profound effects on our lives.

Because we cannot see G1d, we make images of G1d in our minds to explain the spiritual pull that we feel. When we were children, almost all of us pictured G1d as an old man with a long white beard sitting on a throne. Somewhere between 10 and 11 years of age, we jettison that image because it no longer works for us. Throughout our lives we make mental images of what we think G1d is and then throw them out when they no longer satisfy our needs. In between imaginings of G1d, we may become agnostics or atheists. This pattern continues throughout our lives.

I have only convinced one atheist that he believed in G1d, my husband. When I was in surgery, my husband suddenly

---

48   The Christian Old Testament

49   In Hebrew, Jacob used the four letter name of G1d. I have substituted the name, *HaShem* which is used when one is not praying.

felt a deep dread. He felt that I was going to die and he started praying to G1d. He made a deal with G1d that if I lived, he would play bridge, a card game that he hates but I enjoy. When I had recovered sufficiently, he did find a couple with whom we could play bridge and we played weekly for a year. At the end of that time, I told him that he had fulfilled the commitment that he made to G1d. Because he had prayed and kept his commitment, I gently told him that he believed in G1d—and he agreed. By the way, when my husband felt the sense of dread, I was, in fact, near death.

Living in the material world it is easy to cover our soul with our needs, desires, hurts and worries. The thicker the covering, the harder it is to perceive the spark of G1d within us, so, we come to believe that it does not exist. For me physical illness or emotional distress make it much harder to connect with the spark of G1d within me. I am unable to feel G1d's presence when I am sick or in pain. However, because of my mystical experiences, I know that the spiritual dimension exists even when I can not feel it.

However, for my husband waiting for me while I was in surgery, the opposite was true. The strong emotional distress cracked open the covering of his soul and encouraged him to pray and see that G1d was in his life.

I would like to conclude by stating some of the "take-home messages" from this book. The overarching message is: there is more to the world than we can perceive with our senses. This idea can be found in every chapter. In addition to this message, some chapters have additional messages but I did not state them at the end of the chapter because I wanted the reader to find the message that was meaningful to him/her.

The next paragraphs include what I think are the message points from various chapters.

I think there is an important point that is not explicitly stated in Chapter 3. Remember I crossed my fingers behind my back so that I could let G1d know that I could not promise to be Jewish with integrity. Clearly, G1d accepted my doubts; but when my time for exploring other religions was over, G1d sent me a dream telling me to choose Judaism and have a *Bat Mitzvah*. Therefore, G1d not only accepted my doubts but remembered them and let me know when it was time to say the declaration of faith with integrity.

In Chapters 2 and 4, it is very clear that G1d uses messengers—both human and angelic. The experiences written about in Chapter 4 describe two different kinds of G1d's messengers. First, I was sent a dream telling me to warn GS that he was dealing with an unrighteous individual and GS was a messenger to me by explaining to me the meaning of a dream. In the second part of Chapter 4, there was no communication with G1d, rather, my husband and I were in the right place at the right time to help a friend. This incident shows that we never know when G1d is using us to help another person.

For me, the lesson from Chapter 5 is that one can experience the vibrations of one's soul. I have experienced the vibrations of my soul in different ways and doing different activities. The only trick is to pay attention to one's body and recognize odd sensations when they occur.

There are chapters in this book that have far more questions than answers. I have related the mystical experiences that I have had, but that is all I know. I know nothing beyond what is included in this diary nor could I answer the question as to why I have such a strong spiritual pull. I have included mystical experiences of others and they are different than mine. Therefore, it is difficult to develop a common language in which to talk about them.

So, let me conclude with a quote from Shakespeare: "There are more things in Heaven and Earth Horatio, than are dreamt of in your philosophy" (Hamlet Act1 scene 5). Or as I have stated previously, there are more things in the world than we can perceive with our five senses.

I would like to thank *HaShem* for allowing me to have these experiences and gain knowledge of the spiritual dimension.

Special thanks to my husband for his never ending love, his encouragement to write this book and his editing skills.

Thanks to Linda Horn and Linda Altman for editing this manuscript.

Thanks to Elisha Dasenbrock for art lessons and Peggy Nehmen for converting my manuscript into book form and designing the cover of this book.